The Happy Book

BY WELLERAN POLTARNEES

BLUE LANTERN BOOKS
1998

Fifth Printing. Printed in Hong Kong.
ISBN 0-9621131-5-8

Blue Lantern Books
PO Box 4399 • Seattle •Washington
98104-0399

Preface

This book is intended to promote happiness. It was inspired by a series of books written and illustrated by Githa and Millecent Sowerby. Some of the titles were: *The Glad Book, The Joyous Book, The Happy Book, The Merry Book,* and *The Bonny Book*. They were published in England between 1909 and 1918.

I, like the Sowerbys, believe that pictures can powerfully affect ones mood, and that happiness, like any skill, is built by practice.

Happiness is the goal of most people, and yet few of us study the art of happiness. Schools do not offer classes in it, and few of our parents tell us where it is to be found.

In this little book I have collected pictures which make me happy. I have matched them with quotations by philosophers and writers. I think these help us towards the truth about this elusive subject. I have also added my own brief comments, explaining what I had in mind when I put the pictures together.

As slight as it is, I send out this book in the hope that it will cause a little happiness.

W. P.

If there's anything half so much fun as being alive, I'd like to know what it is.
– Frederick Buechner

Sometimes happiness is a simple thing. For no particular reason it rises within us, and we smile or turn cartwheels in our gladness.

A happy family is heaven on earth.
– Russian Proverb

Sharing happiness makes more happiness. There is much to enjoy when we are alone, but when we are together every game is better, every joke is funnier, and every pleasure greater.

The world is so full of a number of things,
I'm sure we should all be as happy as kings.
— Robert Louis Stevenson

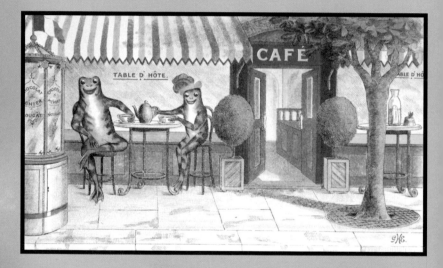

When there is comradeship, little is needed to entertain us. Just talking together, or looking at the things around us, is enough to make us happy.

I want to jump and shout aloud in grati-
tude at having been allowed to live in this
world, sharing with its creatures the
blessed gift of life.

– Malcolm Muggeridge

There is no limit to the amount of happiness we can hold, but sometimes, when we are enormously happy, it swells within us, and we feel as if we were filled with bubbles or balloons, and we must run or leap to let them out.

Creating, acting, changing. That is eternal joy.

– Le Corbusier

Learning is a great source of happiness. In every direction there are things to understand, to learn, to do. Even in a whole lifetime one can never exhaust the opportunities that life presents.

Our highest goal is to serve others.
– Sophocles

    It seems as if our greatest happiness would come from being given what we want. Actually, doing things for others, giving to others, is what gives us the deepest pleasure.

He who gives, teaches me to give.
— Danish Proverb

Receiving a gift makes us happy not only because we are glad to have the gift, but, even more, because we know that someone loved us in the giving.

Write it on your heart that every day is the best day of the year.
      — Ralph Waldo Emerson

Each day is a door waiting to be opened, a continent unexplored.

When one is happy, all things seem possible; even the laws of nature can be ignored.

– Joseph Nelson

Our dreams and our imaginations are an inexhaustible source of inspiration, and give us models of the happiness we seek.

Mental sunshine makes the mind grow,
and perpetual happiness makes human
nature a flower garden in bloom.
*   – Christian D. Larson*

When we feel that what we have is
enough to make us happy, and that all
that surrounds us is as it should be, then
we feel peace. Of all the varieties of happiness this is the loveliest.

Picture Credits

Front Cover
- Alek Plunian. *Histoire de Pommette*, 1920.

Endpapers
- (Front) E. Boyd Smith. *Fun in the Radio World*, 1923.
- (Back) M. Krestjanoff. *Martin And Tommy*, 1920.

Frontispiece
- R.F. von Freyhold. *Bilderbuch*, 1925.

Title page
- M. Foster. *Laughter Land*, n.d.

Copyright page
- Hermann Vogel. *Kinder un Hausmärchen*, circa 1905.

Interior Pages:
- Frank ver Beck. *The Arkansaw Bear*, 1898.
- Ida Waugh. *When Mother was a Little Girl*, circa 1905.
- Marguerite Davis. *The Children's Own Readers*, 1929.
- Harry B. Neilson. *Droll Doings*, circa 1900.
- G.H.E.. *Froggy Folk*, circa 1900.
- Ruth Mary Hallock. *A Child's Garden of Verses*, 1940.
- Peter Newell. *Mother Goose's Menagerie*, 1901.
- Sarah S. Stilwell Weber. *The Saturday Evening Post*, 1918.
- Nellie Farnam & Clarence Biers. *David's Friends at School*, 1936.
- Angusine MacGregor. *The Bunny Book*, 1909.
- Honor C. Appleton. *Josephine's Happy Family*, 1917.
- Charles Robinson. *A Book of Days*, 1901.
- G.H. Thompson. *annual illustration*, circa 1905.
- Stewart Orr. *Two Merry Mariners*, 1902.
- Millicent Sowerby. *A Child's Garden of Verses*, 1908.
- Hyman W. Pertzweig. *annual illustration*, circa 1910.
- Florence Mary Anderson. *The Rainbow Twins*, 1010.
- Artist Unknown. circa 1900.
- Artist Unknown. *Baby in Red Chair(painting)*, circa 1810.

Back cover
- Marie Schubert. *Health Habits*, 1928.